SARAH KORHNAK

The Blogger's Simple Guide to Taxes

A Guide to Saving Time and Money

Contents

Introduction

You have finally done it! Starting a blog has been on your To Do List for quite a while, and you just hit publish on your first post! Congratulations!

Before long, your blog will make its first dollar, and you have already incurred your first blog expenses. Eeeeeek! Now you wonder, "What does the IRS expect me to do about this revenue and these expenses? Am I a business or a hobby? What is tax deductible? What counts as revenue? Is self-employment tax applicable?"

Slow down, slow down. You have lots of questions, and this book will answer them simply and easily. The IRS and your state have lots of rules, but with a little information you can navigate those tax waters without capsizing.

You may be wondering if I'm the right person to help you, so let me tell you about myself. I graduated from college with a B.S. in Accounting, earned my CPA (Certified Public Accountant) license, and worked for 7 years for a public accounting firm that specialized in audit.

Throughout the last decade I have started several small businesses and have been a bookkeeper for many more. For better or worse, the IRS website and I have become well acquainted over the years!

Although the IRS attempts to clearly outline basic tax rules on their website (they actually do a decent job), the rules, exceptions, and accounting jargon can be confusing for people new to small business and the world of taxes and accounting. That's where I come in.

This book will cut through the confusion and explain the tax rules for your blogging business in an easy to understand way. The guidance I provide comes directly from the IRS website, but is summarized for your ease of use, and tailored to your particular type of business. Throughout this book you will find links to the IRS website where a particular topic is discussed. Click on the links to see the IRS information or for additional details on a particular topic.

Like all good books about taxes and accounting, I need to give you a disclaimer! This book is for informational purposes only and does not constitute tax or legal advice. Every tax situation is unique. If you still have nagging questions after reading this book, do your own research on the IRS website or consult a tax accountant. The tax code is lengthy and complicated, but in this book I present accurate, well researched advice using knowledge gained through experience and the resources provided by the IRS. Use your own best judgment when applying this information to your tax situation.

On my website, Small Business Sarah[1] (SmallBusiness-Sarah.com), you can find additional resources for your small business tax and accounting needs. Sign up for my newsletter[2], to receive my free Small Business Startup Checklist.

For additional resources, follow me on Pinterest at Small-BizSarah[3]. I have created Pinterest Boards to provide the best information the web offers on a wide variety of accounting, tax, and small business topics.

Okay, let's get started!

-Sarah

In accordance with IRS Circular 230, we advise you that any discussion of a federal tax issue in this communication is not intended to be used, and cannot be used, by any recipient, for the purpose of avoiding penalties that may be imposed on the recipient under US Federal Tax Laws.

1

So You Started a Blog

Hobby Blog or Business?

It's so exciting! You've posted your first blog post, and your blog is now live. You have wanted to start a blog for ages, and you have finally done it. Congratulations!

After the initial excitement wanes, you may start to panic. What have I gotten myself into? Am I now a business? If I'm a business what do I have to do?

Take a deep yoga breath and stay calm. You may be a business in the eyes of the IRS, or you also may be considered a hobbyist. Let's figure it out, and go from there. This book is here to help you, so there is no need to hyperventilate!

The IRS has nine points[4] for you to consider when determining if your blog is a business or a hobby. The main focus of these nine points is whether or not you are conducting the activity of writing and running the blog with the intention of making a profit. Are you putting the time and effort into it, indicating that you intend to earn money from blogging? Do you have the skill and knowledge necessary to make a profit?

If you started your blog in order to earn money and make a profit, you are a business. If you truly started a blog just for fun (but who are we kidding!), you might be a hobbyist . . . at least for now.

Let's take a closer look at each scenario. First, let's pretend you're a hobby blogger. Are you completely off the hook? Not exactly. If you are writing a blog as a hobby, but your blog makes a little money, you still must report your income on your tax return. Because hobbies still have income reporting requirements, it's important to keep careful records. We'll discuss record-keeping in Chapter 4. Hobby income is reported on Schedule 1 of your 1040 tax return. Although you must report your hobby income to the IRS, you cannot deduct hobby expenses.

If you are a business, you can deduct all of your expenses, even if they exceed the amount of your revenue. This excess loss can offset other types of income that you might have on your tax return, such as income from a regular job. We'll talk more about business expenses later, but one advantage of being a business, is that in a year you have a loss (more expenses than revenue), the loss can help your overall tax picture.

The IRS has a rule that will force you into either the hobby or business category after some years of blogging have elapsed. If you are a hobbyist, but you have had profit from your blog (more revenue than expenses) in 3 of the last 5 tax years, then the IRS determines that you are not a hobby, you are actually a business, regardless of whether you intended to make money from your blog or not. The IRS presumes that an activity is carried on for profit (as a business) if it makes a profit during at least 3 of the last 5 tax years. So even if you began your blog as a hobby, if it turns out your blog makes a profit (more revenue than expenses) in 3 of the last 5 years, then the IRS says that you must begin filing as a business.

This rule works the other way too. If you decide you are a business, but you do **not** have a profit in 3 of the last 5 tax years, the IRS determines that you are not a business, your blog is actually a hobby. Another way to put it, if you are a business, you can only have a loss (expenses that exceed your revenue) for 2 of the last 5 tax years. If you have more than the 2 years of losses, the IRS says that your blog is not a business, but a hobby.

2

Choosing a Business Structure

For the remainder of this book, we're going to assume that your blog is a business. If you are a hobby blogger, some parts of this book will still apply to your situation.

Types of Business Structure

There are five main types of business structure. These are: sole proprietorship, partnership, limited liability company (LLC), S corporation, or corporation. LLCs can be single-member (one person) or multi-member (more than one person, as in a partnership). As a new blogger, the best business structure to choose is either a sole proprietorship or a single-member LLC. These business structures are the simplest to establish and have far fewer requirements and regulations to follow than S corporations or regular corporations.

If you blog with a partner, a partnership or a multi-member LLC will be the easiest formation types. Most bloggers blog on their own, so we'll only discuss the sole proprietorship and single-member LLC business structures here.

A sole proprietorship means that it is just you. You are the business. The business is not a separate legal entity. As a sole proprietor, you will file a Schedule C Profit or Loss from a Business[5] along with your regular personal 1040 Tax Return (the one you file every year). As a sole proprietorship, your business income passes through to your personal income tax return and your business is not taxed separately. Schedule C will calculate your business income or loss for the year, and that figure will carry forward to Schedule 1 of your 1040 Tax Return.

A sole proprietorship is the simplest type of business formation. The drawback of a sole proprietorship is that it offers little in the way of personal asset and legal protection should anything go wrong in your business. The debts of your business belong to you personally, and should a lawsuit arise against your business, the litigant could also pursue your personal assets.

An LLC is a business structure that is created by state statute. LLCs are considered separate legal entities from their members. Although LLCs are separate legal entities, they file their taxes in exactly the same manner as a sole proprietorship. There is no change in tax filings or tax burden. As a single-member LLC, you would file Schedule C along with your 1040 in just the same way that a sole proprietor would. (As an LLC you can elect to be taxed as a corporation if you want to, but believe me, you don't!)

Even though a sole proprietorship and single-member LLC file taxes in exactly the same way, the advantage of forming an LLC is that your personal assets are better protected. Because an LLC is a separate legal entity it shields your personal assets that are separate from your business. Each state differs in how much an LLC shields your personal resources from your business activities. You may never need the added protection that an LLC provides over your personal assets, but it provides a measure of security.

If LLCs file taxes the same way as a sole proprietorship, but provide protection over personal assets, why doesn't everyone automatically set up an LLC? An LLC takes more paperwork to form at the state level and usually costs more in state filing fees. Some states also charge a yearly fee to LLCs. This fee can be several hundred dollars a year.

If you have concerns that legal issues may arise during the course of operating your business, I would recommend speaking with a lawyer to discuss your business formation.

In review, the sole proprietorship and LLC are taxed in exactly the same manner. They are considered pass-through entities. Each year when you file your 1040 tax return by April 15th, now as a business owner you will complete an additional Schedule, the Schedule C. Schedule C calculates your business profit or loss. Your calculated business profit or loss will carry forward to your 1040. Your business income will be combined with your personal income, and the tax amount due calculated. The business is not taxed separately. The tax rate of your business is the same as your personal taxes.

Once you have decided on a business structure, it's time to register your business!

3

Registering Your Business

You've determined your new blog is a business, and you've decided on a business structure. What's next? The next step is to register your business.

Registering with your State

Business formation occurs at the state level, therefore you will first register your business with your state. Do an online search for registering a business in your state, or go to your state's department of revenue or department of state web pages. Begin poking around your state website in order to find information and instructions on business startup forms to file. Each state has different requirements for registering, but there are a few common forms to look for.

Sole Proprietorship

If you have decided to register your business as a sole proprietorship there should be very little paperwork for you to file with your state.

In my state of Pennsylvania there is one major form to register a business and apply for a sales tax licence.

Most sole proprietorships will also need to file a Doing Business As (DBA). This is also referred to as a Fictitious Name. This simply means that you as a sole proprietor are doing business as the name of your blog. For example, you are doing business as Best Blog Ever! If you add another line of work, branch to your business, or another blog, you can file paperwork for additional doing business as names.

If you will be selling merchandise on your blog, your state will probably require you to have a sales tax license. This could be a separate form to be submitted, or it could be included on an overall business registration form.

LLC

When forming an LLC you must choose a name for your LLC. For example, you could name your business Best Blog Ever LLC.

If you think you may eventually expand your business into other areas, you might want to make your LLC name more general. As a wild example, you expand your business to include cleaning houses. You wouldn't want your company called Best Blog Ever LLC in that instance. When you form your LLC, you may want to choose a name that could be applicable for any line of work. For example, choose BBE LLC for your name. Crazy example, but you get the point!

You can file a DBA as an LLC at any time. Back to our example, if you create an LLC called BBE LLC, you would file a DBA stating that BBE LLC is doing business as Best Blog Ever. If you add a house cleaning service at a later time, you could file a DBA stating that BBE LLC is doing business as Best Cleaning Services. This would indicate that BBE LLC was doing business as Best Blog Ever and was also doing business as Best Cleaning Services. Once you have an umbrella LLC created, you can do business as many different names. This is true for the sole proprietorship as well. Your name is the umbrella, and you are doing business as multiple names.

When you choose to register your business as an LLC there will be extra paperwork and most likely extra fees for filing. Your state will likely require you to file a document called Articles of Organization, and perhaps an Operating Agreement. These forms are not difficult to complete. The difficult part is often locating these forms on your state website!

In my experience, state websites do a poor job of easily explaining which forms you need to submit, but the forms themselves (once you locate them!) are not overly complicated or difficult to complete.

Registering with the IRS

You have slogged through your state's website and completed the necessary paperwork to register your business in your state. Now you may wonder if the IRS registration process is going to be even worse. Nope. It's easier!

Business formation happens at the state level. You still need to pay taxes at the federal level but you don't need to file extra paperwork to register your business at the federal level.

Once your business is up and running, at the end of the year, you'll complete the Schedule C, Profit or Loss from Business, along with your personal tax return, the 1040. You will complete the Schedule C if you are a sole proprietorship or an LLC. At the top of Schedule C is a little box where you check that this is an initial return. Checking this box lets the IRS know that you are a new business. That's it, amazingly simple!

Do I need an EIN?

An EIN (Employer Identification Number) is an identifying number for each business, similar to a social security number for a person.

If you are a sole proprietorship or a single member LLC, you are not required to have an EIN.

If you are a partnership, a corporation, or have employees then you must obtain an EIN.

Although a sole proprietorship and single member LLC are not required to have an EIN, you can obtain an EIN if you wish. This is something I do recommend. As a business owner you may come across applications or forms that require you to give your business ID. Your social security number can suffice in many of these situations in place of an EIN, however you may prefer not to provide your social security number more than is absolutely necessary. Having an EIN in this situation will allow you to keep your social security number private.

As a business owner you may run across situations where an EIN is mandatory, such as opening wholesale accounts or signing up for affiliate programs. It's convenient to already have this step completed.

The process of getting an EIN[6] is surprisingly easy. The IRS has an online form that immediately gives you an EIN after asking a few question about your business. I recommend that you go ahead and get an EIN for your business.

4

Business Recordkeeping

As discussed earlier, whether your blog is a hobby or a business, you still need to keep financial records. Both hobbies that earn money and businesses must report financial information to the IRS.

First Steps

The first step is to establish a bank account and credit card exclusively for your business activities. The financial transactions of your business should be kept separate from your personal financial transactions. You should have a separate bank account and credit card that is only used for business purposes.

One way to keep your business financial transactions separate is to dedicate an existing personal bank account and credit card for business activities. For example, when my husband

and I got married we had two bank accounts, after combining our finances we only used one bank account for our personal financial transactions. That "extra" bank account that wasn't being used could have become my dedicated account for business transactions. This method can accommodate your needs in the early days of business ownership before you make the commitment to open bank accounts in the name of your business.

The best way to obtain separate business financial accounts is to open up a bank account, and credit or debit card, in the name of your business. Your local branch will have information on opening a business checking account. Going online for all of your business banking needs is also an option. Some people choose only to use PayPal for their business income and a PayPal debit card for their expenses. Capital One also has online business checking accounts that are easy to set up. Business accounts vary in fees and minimum balance requirements, so look carefully at the fee schedule before opening an account.

Whatever method you choose, keep business transactions completely separate from your personal money.

If you start out as a hobby blogger, I still recommend maintaining separate financial accounts for your blogging transactions for several reasons. First, even if your blog is just for fun, it's helpful to know how much money you are sinking into your hobby. As the expenses of your blog accumulate and your designated blog money diminishes, that immediate information can help you make better decisions about your hobby blog. Second, you still have to report your hobby income to the IRS, so keeping your blog money separate will make calculating those figures much easier at the end of the year.

It's easy to become lax about separating business money from personal money, but it is so important to do. A reputable business does not mingle business and personal funds. If the IRS performs an audit and sees that business money has been mixed in with personal money, it could influence whether or not the IRS views you as a legitimate business. If the IRS is auditing your business and finds business transactions mingled with personal spending, they may audit your personal tax return as well. In some states, if you mingle personal money with business it can erode the financial protection a LLC provides.

Keeping a separation between business and personal money makes it easier to financially analyze your blogging business, and makes the bookkeeping for your business much simpler. All around, financial separation between your blogging business finances and your personal finances is a smart idea.

When you start your blogging business, you need to save all of your business receipts. Some of your receipts may be physical receipts from a store, but many will be electronic receipts that are emailed to you. Save all of your electronic receipts in one email folder so that you can immediately access them as needed.

To satisfy the IRS, you will also need access to your business bank statements. Sometimes there are fees for receiving a physical bank statement in the mail. If you choose not to receive paper statements in the mail, be sure you will have access to your online bank statements for at least 3 years after you file the related tax return. In almost every situation, the IRS stipulates that keeping your records for 3 years after you file your tax return is sufficient.

According to the IRS, the burden of proof is on the taxpayer to prove and validate all income and expenses reported on a tax return.

Bookkeeping

As a new business owner, if the number of transactions occurring monthly is minimal, having your business money segregated from your personal money may be enough. With few transactions, all of the data needed for your tax return will be on your bank statement or credit card statement. After summarizing your statements, you may have all the data you need to complete your end of year tax return. This bookkeeping system works only when the number of monthly transactions is minimal and the business transactions are separate from personal transactions.

As your business grows, the next step may be using a spreadsheet to track monthly income and expenses. Each transaction can be assigned a category such as Affiliate Revenue or Supplies Expense for easy sorting and summarizing at the end of the year. Again, this method is best when the transactions are few, and business money is kept separate from personal.

The best and easiest way to keep track of income and expenses is to use an online accounting program. There are many good options to choose from, and most have a free or low-cost version. Online accounting programs include QuickBooks, Freshbooks, the Wave App, Xero, or GoDaddy bookkeeping. Most of these programs will automatically import bank and credit card transactions which is a huge time saver. These programs also memorize transactions, and can automatically post new transactions to the right category. These automatic functions can make bookkeeping almost effortless.

My recommendation is to use QuickBooks Online Simple Start. QuickBooks provides a quality product at a reasonable price. Their program is easy to use, creates accurate results, and can grow with your business. You can find a tutorial on how to get started with QuickBooks on my website.

Whatever method you choose for your bookkeeping, they all work best when you maintain them on a monthly basis!

By setting up your bookkeeping system in the early days of your business you will save time and stress at tax time.

In addition, by keeping accurate and timely financial records, you can make educated decisions that will help grow your blogging business. By pulling up your financial reports you can quickly analyze your business cash flow. Are your expenses higher than you thought? What area of revenue is performing the best? Is one function of your business costing you more than another? Solid financial data will reveal patterns that aid in decision making. When you make informed decisions, you save money and increase revenues! That sounds like a recipe for success!

5

Schedule C

We have mentioned Schedule C several times. Now let's take an in-depth look at Schedule C.

When you file your Schedule C for the first time, there are some questions at the top of the page that you will need to answer. Let's cover a few of the questions that could be most confusing. Your tax program and the IRS Instructions to Schedule C can also help if you are still unsure.

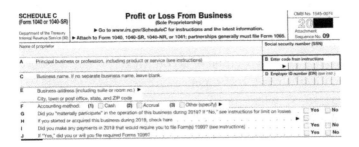

At the end of your first year in business, you'll file Schedule C along with your personal tax return. At the top of Schedule C, find line H, and simply check the box that you started the business during the year. Now the IRS knows that you are a new business. No other type of business registration is required at the federal level for a sole proprietorship or single member LLC.

Cash vs. Accrual

The first question that might be difficult to understand is line F, selecting your accounting method. You can choose between Cash, Accrual, or Other.

The Cash method of accounting is the easiest for small business owners to implement and understand. The Cash Method of accounting dictates that you record revenue when money is deposited in your bank account, and you record expenses when money leaves your bank account. This may seem obvious, but the nuances will become clear when I explain the Accrual Method of accounting.

With the Accrual Method of accounting, revenue is recorded when it is earned, and expenses are recorded when they are incurred. So what's the difference between this and the cash method of accounting? Let me explain with an example.

It's December 31st and you complete a sponsored post, post it to your blog, and complete all required social media tasks per your agreement. Your agreement with the sponsoring company is for $200 in exchange for your post and other social media requirements. You have completed your end of the agreement as of 12/31. The sponsor doesn't make the payment until they get back to work on January 2nd. With the Cash Method of accounting, you would record the revenue in January because that is when the cash arrived in your bank account. With the Accrual Method of accounting, you would record the revenue on December 31st, because you completed the work, fulfilled your part of the agreement, and effectively earned the revenue on that day.

For most small businesses the cash basis of accounting is the most straightforward and easiest to understand, and therefore is a good choice when selecting your accounting method.

Material Participation

The next Schedule C question you will come across is on line G, "Did you materially participate in the operation of the business?"

There is a long list of questions that the IRS uses to determine material participation, but usually, material participation can be determined after answering just the first few. For the full list of questions refer to Schedule C Instructions[7].

The first question asks "Did I (plus my spouse if they are involved) work more than 500 hours during the year in the business?" For ease of calculation, this breaks down to about 10 hours per week. If the answer is yes, you materially participated in the business.

If you don't meet the requirement of the first question, then the next question is, "Do I do most of the work?" Even if you didn't work 500 hours, but your work is the only activity in the business, then you did materially participate. This scenario applies to most sole proprietorships or single-member LLCs without employees.

Those two questions usually allow you to meet the material participation rule. If you don't meet the requirement after those questions, use your tax software or the instructions to Schedule C to look up the other questions that might allow you to check the box to say that yes you did materially participate.

Why is being able to say you materially participated important? If you did not materially participate in the business, the IRS may consider your business to be a passive activity. If it is a passive activity, then you may not be able to count business losses against other types of income. It's in your best interest to be able to say you materially participated.

1099

The final question that may have you scratching your head is question I, "Did you make payments that would require you to file 1099s?"

The 1099 is an informational form that the IRS uses to make sure the revenue that people and businesses earn is accounted for and reported to the IRS. For a blogger, the most likely reason you would need to file 1099s is if you paid independent contractors for services they performed for you during the year. These are not employees, but individuals you hire to perform certain duties. Many bloggers employ Virtual Assistants (VAs) for graphic design, video editing, or general administrative work. These VA's are not employees but are independent contractors. For each VA whom you paid more than $600 in a year, you must file a Form 1099-MISC. There is one exception to this rule. If you paid your VA via a third party processor such as PayPal, you are not required to file a 1099. Instead, a 1099-K will be filed by the third-party processor if certain criteria are met.

Part I and II

The remainder of Schedule C is for recording your business income, your business expenses, and determining your overall business profit or loss. We'll be discussing Expenses and Revenue in the next sections.

Part I	**Income**		
1	Gross receipts or sales. See instructions for line 1 and check the box if this income was reported to you on Form W-2 and the "Statutory employee" box on that form was checked ▶ ☐	1	
2	Returns and allowances	2	
3	Subtract line 2 from line 1	3	
4	Cost of goods sold (from line 42)	4	
5	**Gross profit.** Subtract line 4 from line 3	5	
6	Other income, including federal and state gasoline or fuel tax credit or refund (see instructions)	6	
7	**Gross income.** Add lines 5 and 6 ▶	7	

Part II Expenses. Enter expenses for business use of your home **only** on line 30.

8	Advertising	8		18	Office expense (see instructions)	18
9	Car and truck expenses (see instructions)	9		19	Pension and profit-sharing plans	19
				20	Rent or lease (see instructions):	
10	Commissions and fees	10		a	Vehicles, machinery, and equipment	20a
11	Contract labor (see instructions)	11		b	Other business property	20b
12	Depletion	12		21	Repairs and maintenance	21
13	Depreciation and section 179 expense deduction (not included in Part III) (see instructions)	13		22	Supplies (not included in Part III)	22
				23	Taxes and licenses	23
				24	Travel and meals:	
14	Employee benefit programs (other than on line 19)	14		a	Travel	24a
15	Insurance (other than health)	15		b	Deductible meals (see instructions)	24b
16	Interest (see instructions):			25	Utilities	25
a	Mortgage (paid to banks, etc.)	16a		26	Wages (less employment credits)	26
b	Other	16b		27a	Other expenses (from line 48)	27a
17	Legal and professional services	17		b	Reserved for future use	27b

28	**Total expenses** before expenses for business use of home. Add lines 8 through 27a ▶	28	
29	Tentative profit or (loss). Subtract line 28 from line 7	29	
30	Expenses for business use of your home. Do not report these expenses elsewhere. Attach Form 8829 unless using the simplified method (see instructions). **Simplified method filers only:** enter the total square footage of: (a) your home: _____ and (b) the part of your home used for business: _____ Use the Simplified Method Worksheet in the instructions to figure the amount to enter on line 30	30	
31	**Net profit or (loss).** Subtract line 30 from line 29.		
	• If a profit, enter on both **Schedule 1 (Form 1040 or 1040-SR), line 3** (or **Form 1040-NR, line 13**) and on **Schedule SE, line 2.** (If you checked the box on line 1, see instructions). Estates and trusts, enter on **Form 1041, line 3.**	31	
	• If a loss, you **must** go to line 32.		
32	If you have a loss, check the box that describes your investment in this activity (see instructions).		
	• If you checked 32a, enter the loss on both **Schedule 1 (Form 1040 or 1040-SR), line 3** (or **Form 1040-NR, line 13**) and on **Schedule SE, line 2.** (If you checked the box on line 1, see the line 31 instructions). Estates and trusts, enter on **Form 1041, line 3.**	32a ☐ All investment is at risk. 32b ☐ Some investment is not at risk.	
	• If you checked 32b, you **must** attach **Form 6198.** Your loss may be limited.		

6

Blogging Revenue

At its most basic, cash coming in equals revenue. Simple, right? Most of the time it is simple, but occasionally it is a little tricky. Let's talk about each type of revenue you may receive from your blogging activities.

Affiliate Income

Affiliate Income can be a major source of revenue for bloggers. When you sign up for an affiliate program, you are given a special link to use when referencing products from a certain company. Each time one of your readers clicks on your special affiliate link and makes a purchase, you receive a small portion of the purchase price. A win for everyone! All of your affiliate sales are revenue and should be reported on your tax return.

Ad Revenue

Ads are another common source of income for bloggers. When you place ads on your site and readers click on those ads, you get paid by the ad network. All payments to you from the ad network is revenue to your blogging business.

Product Sales

If you have created your own product which you offer for sale on your blog or on another website, all sales are income to your business, but any expenditures you incur in creating your product are also recorded as expenses.

Sponsored Posts

Many bloggers also participate in sponsored posts. You agree to talk about a product or company on your blog or on your social media platforms in exchange for compensation. If your compensation is money, then that is revenue that should be recorded.

What if you receive merchandise in exchange for your blog post and social media mentions? In this case the Fair Market Value

(FMV) of the merchandise you received should be counted as revenue. FMV is just a fancy way of saying what the item costs if you were to buy it in a store.

The IRS views income as anything received in exchange for products or services. If you are performing a service for a company by blogging about their product, whether they pay you in cash or with "free" product, it's still income. When you make an agreement to do something in exchange for something else, make sure the related revenue is recorded in whatever form it might take, be it revenue in the form of cash or revenue in the form of product.

Free Items

As a blogger you may occasionally be sent products for you to enjoy, eBooks for you to read, or samples for you to try. Many of these will unexpectedly show up at your door or in your email inbox as companies try to reach influencers with their brand and products. If small dollar items are sent to you, without any understanding that you will do something in return, the FMV value of that item does not need to be recorded as income. When another blogger sends you a $2.99 eBook via email and you have not agreed to do anything in exchange for receiving the eBook, there is no need to record $2.99 as revenue in your accounting records. Items you receive that are not in exchange for services or are not part of an agreement do not need to be recorded as revenue.

Giveaway Items

Most bloggers will at some point host giveaways. Often with giveaways, the product being given away is donated to the blogger. The item you receive is revenue to you, because it is in exchange for your services, hosting the giveaway. However, the item is also an expense because ultimately you give it to someone else, the winner! In this instance the net tax effect is zero, and for simplicity, I would not record either the revenue or the related expense. However, technically the IRS would probably prefer that you show both the income and the expense, even though their bottom line is not affected either way!

As a blogger, your income will be reported on Schedule C Part I, line 1.

Part I	Income		
1	Gross receipts or sales. See instructions for line 1 and check the box if this income was reported to you on Form W-2 and the "Statutory employee" box on that form was checked ▶ ☐	1	
2	Returns and allowances	2	
3	Subtract line 2 from line 1	3	
4	Cost of goods sold (from line 42)	4	
5	**Gross profit.** Subtract line 4 from line 3	5	
6	Other income, including federal and state gasoline or fuel tax credit or refund (see instructions)	6	
7	**Gross income.** Add lines 5 and 6 ▶	7	

7

Blogging Expenses

Before we begin discussing the different and specific types of expenses you might encounter while blogging, let's first discuss some general information about expenses.

Understanding Expenses

In layman's terms, an expense is something that you spend money on. Fairly simple.

A deductible expense is an IRS allowable expense that can be deducted from your business revenue on your tax return.

According to the IRS Publication 535[8], "To be deductible, a business expense must be both ordinary and necessary. An ordinary expense is one that is common and accepted in your industry. A necessary expense is one that is helpful and appropriate for your trade or business. An expense does not have to be indispensable to be considered necessary."

To be considered tax deductible and expense must be considered both ordinary and necessary in the eyes of the IRS. The IRS further explains that ordinary means it is common in your industry, so in your case, it must be an expense which is ordinary to blogging. Do other bloggers commonly have the same type of expenditures? To be necessary it merely has to be part of conducting your business, it has to be helpful to you as you earn money from your blog.

The rules for what constitutes a deductible business expense are broad, but don't use that to take advantage of the system. Personal expenses should never be included with your business expenses.

As a small business owner the line between business and personal use of an item can become blurred. For example, you might use a printer to test print your opt-in freebie, and the very next instant use the same printer to print a coupon for the grocery store!

When you purchase something that is used for both business and personal use, be sure to only take the business portion as a tax deduction. For example, you might decide you use the printer about 75% of the time for business and 25% of the time for your home. Only take 75% of the cost of the printer as a tax deduction, not the full 100%.

Supplies and Materials

Many business expenses that bloggers incur are similar to other businesses and as such are clearly deductible. However, when it comes to the supplies and materials that bloggers purchase for their projects and posts, the waters get a little murky.

Most blog niches, (DIY, home décor, and food just to name a few) rely on blog posts with a project focus. Spending money on supplies is necessary in order to offer tested instructions and beautiful step by step photos to your readers. All the supplies, materials, and ingredients for blog projects can really add up! How much can you treat as a business expense? What can you deduct on your taxes?

Although the IRS tax code covers many topics in depth, they have yet to publish any definitive guidance to bloggers on how to specifically handle many of the financial situations that bloggers encounter every day. In the absence of situational specific guidance, we must lean on general tax advice to determine what constitutes a business expenses for bloggers.

The general tax guidance supplied by the IRS tells us to ask whether an expense is ordinary and necessary.

The other area related to blogging expenses where extra care should be taken is determining whether an expense is truly for a business purpose, or whether it has a personal use as well. Some items are both personal and business related, and the IRS does allow you to pro-rate and deduct the business portion on your tax return.

Supplies and Materials Expense Examples

Discussing a few examples will be the easiest way to understand when blogging supplies and materials are tax deductible.

Let's say you are a home décor DIY blogger who is painting a table you bought at a thrift store. You are taking step by step photos as you go along, and do a nice post about the table when you are done. The table then becomes a permanent fixture in your home. There are several things to consider when deciding what is tax deductible in this scenario. Many of the supplies required to repaint the table are tax deductible. These materials were an ordinary and necessary expense in order for you to blog about fixing up the table. These materials might include sand paper, primer, or paint. Any left-over materials likely will be used on future blog projects. Therefore, I would include the refinishing supplies and materials as fully tax deductible.

Determining whether or not the table itself is tax deductible gets trickier. Although the table was ordinary and necessary for your blog post project, you now use the table everyday so it certainly has a personal component. You might consider allocating only a portion of the cost of the table as a business expense. However, if you are a blogger that fixes up furniture and then sells it, or you give the table away when finished, then the entire cost of the table would likely be tax deductible. This portion of the puzzle has no straightforward answer. You will have to make a judgement call to the best of your ability based in large part on how the table is used after the project is completed.

Looking at another example, let's say you are a food blogger who only blogs about cake. Each time you go to the grocery store, the groceries you buy for your family are **not** tax deductible. The groceries you buy to feed your family are personal and not business related. Having a food blog doesn't mean all of your groceries are business expenses! If you purchase ingredients to make your famous German Chocolate Cake, and you then blog about the cake you made from those specifically purchased ingredients, then your supplies would be tax deductible.

Let's take this a step further. Imagine that your son is having a birthday party, and you need several cakes to feed everyone at the party. You have a brilliant idea and plan to make your famous German Chocolate Cake for the party and then blog about the cake. One cake won't be enough, so you buy ingredients for three of your famous German Chocolate Cakes. It is tempting to include the cost of ingredients for all three cakes as a business expense, but in reality only the ingredients for **one** cake are tax deductible. In order to blog about your cake, you only need one cake for step by step instructions and pictures. The remaining two cakes were necessary only on a personal level, and therefore the supplies for those cakes are not tax deductible.

Err on the side of caution. Don't push the envelope to see what you can get away with. Be conservative as you determine what is ordinary and necessary for your blog, and what is for personal or business use.

Keep Excellent Records

When purchasing blog post materials and supplies, record keeping is extremely important. When you purchase the ingredients for your German Chocolate Cake along with your families groceries for the week, pay for the German Chocolate Cake items in a separate transaction, and preferably with a business only credit or debit card. Jot down on your separate receipt what the materials or ingredients were for, and possibly even mark down the date the blog post went live. The more information you can provide to substantiate that these items were for business purposes, the better.

What About Sponsored Posts?

In the case of a project you do as part of a sponsored post, you can make an even stronger argument that the supplies and materials expenses you incurred were ordinary, necessary, and purely business related. Expenses incurred for the direct production of revenue are deductible, and often these purchases are not items you will continue to use personally. These are items you needed in order to complete the project and get paid by the sponsoring company.

I wish I was able to give you a much more straightforward answer concerning every supplies and materials purchase, but I hope you now have the tools to judge for yourself which items are deductible on your tax return. Each bloggers' situation will be different because of what they blog about, and each post will need to be evaluated based on the IRS criteria for business expenses. Remember to ask, is the expense ordinary, necessary, and not of a personal nature?

Other Expenses

The following two chapters will discuss other specific blog expense topics such as travel and home office. But before we move on to those topics, let's look at all of the deductible expense categories on Schedule C, including those we haven't discussed and briefly go over what type of expenses will apply to each category.

Part II	Expenses. Enter expenses for business use of your home **only** on line 30.				
8	Advertising	8		18	Office expense (see instructions)	18
9	Car and truck expenses (see instructions)	9		19	Pension and profit-sharing plans	19
				20	Rent or lease (see instructions):	
10	Commissions and fees	10		a	Vehicles, machinery, and equipment	20a
11	Contract labor (see instructions)	11		b	Other business property	20b
12	Depletion	12		21	Repairs and maintenance	21
13	Depreciation and section 179 expense deduction (not included in Part III) (see instructions)	13		22	Supplies (not included in Part III)	22
				23	Taxes and licenses	23
				24	Travel and meals:	
14	Employee benefit programs (other than on line 19)	14		a	Travel	24a
15	Insurance (other than health)	15		b	Deductible meals (see instructions)	24b
16	Interest (see instructions):			25	Utilities	25
a	Mortgage (paid to banks, etc.)	16a		26	Wages (less employment credits)	26
b	Other	16b		27a	Other expenses (from line 48)	27a
17	Legal and professional services	17		b	Reserved for future use	27b

Advertising - Facebook Ads, Promoted Pins, possibly giveaway items, or any other type of advertising

Car and Truck - your calculated mileage expense plus parking, meters, and tolls as discussed in the Travel Expenses chapter

Commissions and fees - affiliate commissions you pay, PayPal fees, bank fees, etc.

Contract labor - amounts you pay to virtual assistants. You will record any amount paid to every assistant who did work for you. If you paid your virtual assistant less than $600 you still record the payment as a business expense here, but you will not need to file a 1099.

Depletion - not applicable for a blogger (deals with timber or mineral rights)

Depreciation and section 179 expense - for major asset purchases only

Employee benefit programs - not applicable to you until you hire employees

Insurance - if you bought liability insurance for your business, but most likely will not apply

Interest - credit card interest or if you purchased a building, mortgage interest

Legal and Professional Services - hiring a lawyer to file forms or an accountant to do your bookkeeping and taxes

Office Expenses - the items you use every day such as paper and ink, this is a broad category that covers many items

Pension and profit-sharing - not applicable unless you have employees

Rent or Lease - only if you rent office space or other equipment for your business

Repairs and Maintenance - this usually applies if you own or rent office space, and is not applicable for repairs or maintenance of a qualified home office space

Supplies - as a blogger, this could be a category you use often for blog project materials

Taxes and licenses – the cost of your business registration would apply here

Travel, Meals, and Entertainment – hotels, travel and business meals, etc as discussed in the Travel Expenses chapter

Utilities - if you rent or buy a separate office space, the utilities for that space would go here

Wages - if you have employees

Other Expenses - this category is used to capture anything not already covered by the categories above

The calculation and deduction for the Business Use of Your Home tax deduction goes after the calculation of revenue minus expenses on line 30. That tax deduction will be discussed in a later chapter.

8

Travel Expenses

As your blog continues to grow, you might decide to attend a blogging conference. How fun! But what travel expenses are tax deductible?

Travel Expenses

The IRS defines travel expenses as the ordinary and necessary expense of traveling away from home for your business profession or job. This is travel away from your tax home, which is defined by the IRS as your principal place of business.

As a blogger, traveling to conferences related to your blog or business, certainly qualifies as a deductible travel expense based upon the IRS guidelines. This is not the only type of travel that is a deductible expense, but it is probably the most common for a blogger. Apply the IRS standard of ordinary and necessary to your individual business travel expenses to determine if they qualify as a tax deduction.

Travel Expense Details

Now that you have concluded that your travel is ordinary and necessary for your business, let's dig into the details of your travel and the portion that is deductible. We'll use the example of attending a blogging conference.

First, the cost of your conference ticket is tax deductible.

If you travel by air or train you can deduct the cost of the plane or train ticket. If you rent a car, you can deduct that cost.

If you drive your own car you can use the standard mileage rate. I'll cover business mileage expense in more depth later in this chapter.

If you need to stay overnight, you can deduct the cost of the hotel room. However, if you use rewards points for your hotel or airfare, and did not actually spend money, you cannot deduct those as a business expense.

Other ordinary and necessary expenses of travel such as taxis, tips, and parking are also tax deductible.

Meals

Meals while traveling are an exception. Meals are subject to a 50% limit. If you are traveling away from your tax home, and you purchase a meal while you are traveling, only 50% of the cost is allowed as a tax deduction. This holds true for non-traveling business meals as well. If you and your partners have a business meeting at a restaurant, only 50% of the cost is deductible as a business expense.

If you are legitimately traveling for business, you can deduct all of your expenses. Meals are the only exception with the 50% limit.

Remember to hold on to your receipts and keep careful records when you travel!

If you love reading legal speak and want to dive into this topic further, the IRS outlines these guidelines in Publication 463[9].

Business Mileage

Another often missed business tax deduction is mileage. When you use your personal vehicle for a business purpose, those miles can translate into a deduction on your tax return. Tax deductions equal money in your pocket! The IRS lays out all the details in Publication 463[10](which is rather lengthy and boring) so let me fill you in on the details!

What counts as business mileage?

Here are some examples of business miles you might drive as a blogger:

Driving to the store to pick up supplies for a blog project
Driving to the post office to mail a giveaway prize
Going to the post office to check your business P.O. Box
Driving to a business planning meeting
Attending a business conference

Any miles you drive in your personal car for a business purpose count toward a deduction on your tax return.

The IRS understands that when you drive your personal vehicle for a business purpose, it is costing you money in wear and tear on your vehicle and for the gasoline used. The cost to you is considered a business expense on your tax return. To calculate this business expense, the IRS has set up a standard mileage rate. The standard mileage rate represents what you spend to drive each mile. The standard mileage set by the IRS rate changes each year and is based on the price of gas and other inflationary calculations. For example, in 2021 the standard mileage rate was 56 cents per mile (.56).

To find the current year standard mileage rate set by the IRS go to https://www.irs.gov/tax-professionals/standard-mileage-rates[11].

Here is an example of how it works. If you drove 100 business miles with your personal car in 2021, 100 x .56 = $56.00 This represents a business expense you incurred and can be included on your tax return with your other business expenses.

How should you track and record your business miles?

The IRS expects you to maintain timely records by keeping a log that documents any miles driven in your personal car for business purposes. Your log should include:

- Date
- Beginning and ending odometer readings
- Calculation of miles driven
- Destination name and location
- The business purpose of your trip
- Other expenses incurred such as parking or tolls

I have created a business mileage log[12] for you. Print it out and keep it in your car, so that you don't miss any business miles your drive.

At the end of the year, add up all of your business miles driven and multiply that by the IRS standard mileage rate.

All other expenses such as parking, tolls, and meters can be totaled and included as an expense on your tax return. In most cases the IRS wants you to have a receipt of every business expense. However, the IRS recognizes that sometimes a receipt is unavailable. They have made an exception and still allow a deduction when receipts are not available and the transaction is less than $75. A receipt is not possible for certain transactions such as meters or tolls, and this is why recording these expenses on your mileage log is so important. The log serves as the documentation of these expenses.

Where should you include mileage expense on your tax return?

Your calculated mileage expense plus parking, tolls, and other expenses are included on line 9 of Schedule C.

Tracking your business mileage is easy and will help you keep more money in your pocket!

9

Home Office and QBI Tax Deductions

There are two special tax deductions you need to pay attention to as a blogging business. If you qualify, they can help save you money when paying your taxes.

Home Office

As a home based business owner and blogger, you may qualify for business use of your home tax deduction, often referred to as the home office tax deduction. Let's walk you through this often overlooked tax deduction.

When determining if you qualify for a home office tax deduction, the main question to ask yourself is, "Do I **regularly** use part of my home **exclusively** for conducting business?"

Exclusively

The space where you conduct your business can range from a table, an actual office room in your home, or even an entire floor of your home. The size of the business space that could qualify for the home office tax deduction is irrelevant. What does matter is how you use the space.

To qualify for a home office tax deduction, the IRS stipulates that you cannot use the space for both business and personal purposes, it must be used only for business purposes. If you have a home office, you can **only** use it for the business to qualify for the tax deduction. I personally have half of my basement that I use exclusively for my Etsy shop. This portion of my basement houses all of my inventory and packaging supplies and it's where I process all of my orders. I don't use that portion of my basement for anything else but running my Etsy shop, so it meets the exclusivity test.

As a blogger, it may be more difficult to meet the exclusivity test.

If you are a food blogger, your kitchen does not qualify for business use of your home tax deduction because you are using your kitchen for both personal and business activities. If you had two kitchens in your house, and you used one exclusively to make and test your food blog recipes, then that second kitchen would qualify for a home office tax deduction.

While writing this book, I am doing most of my work at the

kitchen table or on the family room couch. Because the kitchen table and couch are not exclusively used for the business, those areas of my house don't qualify for a tax deduction.

An area of your home that you use to store business inventory does count for the business use of your home tax deduction, as long as it isn't used for storing other items (such as a pantry containing your food blog supplies and family groceries). So if on your blog you sell merchandise that you store in your home, the part of your home where you store your merchandise and inventory would qualify for the business use of your home tax deduction.

Regularly

If you have an area of your home that you use exclusively for your business, you must also use that area regularly in order to qualify for the business use of your home tax deduction. It can't be an area of your home that you only occasionally use for the business. The IRS does not specify how often you must use the business area of your home in order to meet their "regularly" requirement, so use your best judgment.

Principal Place of Business

The IRS also stipulates that your home must be your principal place of business in order to take the home office tax deduction. As a blogger, this is almost always the case as blogging is usually a home based business.

Calculating the Home Office Tax Deduction

If you use part of your home regularly and exclusively for your blog and qualify for a home office tax deduction, there are two methods to choose from when calculating the amount of your tax deduction. The Actual Expenses method is the most difficult and time-consuming. The Simplified Method is very simple and easy to calculate.

To calculate your home office tax deduction for either method, begin by calculating the square footage of the business-use part of your home. In our example, our business portion is a 10×10 area or 100 square feet. Next, determine the square footage of your entire house, for this example, we will assume you have a 1,000 square foot home. Lastly, calculate the percentage used for business purposes, so for our example, 100 sf/1,000 sf= 10% of the home is used for business purposes.

Now let's take a closer look at both methods.

Actual Expenses Method

With the Actual Expenses Method, a portion of the expenses involved in owning and maintaining your home can be counted as a business tax deduction. In our example, 10% of real estate taxes, insurance, mortgage interest, utilities, depreciation, etc. can be counted as a home office tax deduction. These are called Indirect Expenses.

There can also be direct expenses. If you have to paint or repair the exclusively business portion of your house, then the entire cost to repair or maintain that area is a business expense. However if you are repairing or maintaining other parts of your home, those expenses are unrelated, and not even a portion can be taken as a business expense. For instance if you paint or repair your kitchen, you can't claim even a portion of that as a business expense because those costs are unrelated to the business portion of your home.

If you choose the Actual Expenses method, you'll need to complete Form 8829[13]. This may seem confusing, but remember that you should be using a tax professional or tax software to complete your tax return. The tax program will walk you through these steps and complete this form for you. You just need to know to check that box that yes, you do qualify for a home office/business use of your home deduction.

There are limits on how much of a home office deduction you can take based on your business profits for the year. These limits are calculated on Form 8829. The tax program you use will also adjust your Schedule A itemized deductions (if you itemize) for the portion of certain items (such as real estate taxes) you take as a business deduction. The IRS is not going to let you count the same expenses twice.

The Simplified Method

Yes, there really is a simplified method, and it's simple!

Once again, begin by calculating the square footage of the business use of your home. Let's use our 10×10 foot example, which is 100 square feet. Multiply the business square footage by $5 to determine your tax deduction. In our example of a 100 square feet home office that's a $500 tax deduction. The maximum deduction for the simplified method is 300 square feet or $1,500. Isn't that easy? The Simplified Method calculation is right on Schedule C.

There is a gross income limitation on the easy method. If you don't have enough profit to cover the business use of your home tax deduction, you're not going to be able to take it in that year. So if your profit (revenue-expenses = profit) was only $100, you can only take up to $100 of the home office tax deduction. You can't take the home office tax deduction if it will cause you to have a business loss in that year.

If you are enthralled by this riveting topic and want to know more, the IRS explains the guidelines for the business use of your home in Publication 587[14].

Qualified Business Income (QBI) Tax Deduction

The Qualified Business Income (QBI) tax deduction first became available for the 2018 tax year as part of the Tax Cuts and Job Acts. It allows eligible pass-through small businesses, like sole-proprietorships and LLCs, to deduct up to 20% of their qualified business income on their taxes.

Qualified business income is "the net amount of qualified items of income, gain, deduction and loss with respect to any trade or business." In laymen's terms this just means the net income, revenues minus expenses, of your business. The QBI therefore lower's the amount of business income you will pay taxes on by 20%.

Not paying taxes on 20% of your business net income is a huge benefit!

There are certain types of income that are excluded, such as interest income, capital gains, and income earned outside the United States. However, most of the excluded items will not apply to a blogging business. And like many tax deductions, if your income is too high, you may not qualify.

To claim the deduction you will need to complete and attach Form 8995, *Qualified Business Income Deduction Simplified Com-*

putation, or Form 8995-A, *Qualified Business Income Deduction to your tax return.* This form will help you calculate the amount of your deduction. The result will then be carried forward to page 1 of your 1040 tax return.

If you hire a tax preparer to complete your tax return, ask the question and make sure they are claiming the QBI deduction for you. Don't miss out on this great opportunity for tax savings!

10

Self-Employment

Self-Employment Tax

When you work for an employer, your pay stub reflects the portion of taxes withheld from your paycheck for Social Security and Medicare. What you may not know is that in addition to the Social Security and Medicare tax you pay, your employer also pays an equal portion on your behalf.

As a self-employed small business owner, there is no employer to pay the employer portion of the Social Security and Medicare tax for you. This is now your responsibility. This is referred to as the self-employment tax.

The self-employment tax applies to anyone who has their own business, including a sole proprietorship, a partnership, or an LLC.

To determine if you need to pay self-employment tax, begin by completing your Schedule C business tax form as usual. If your Schedule C shows a profit of $400 or more for the year, you may be required to pay the self-employment tax. The amount of self-employment tax you owe will be calculated on Schedule SE[15].

I know, forms, forms, and more forms, but if you are using a tax program, the program is going to see that the self-employment tax was triggered by your responses and walk you through completing your Schedule SE.

The self-employment portion of business taxes you owe also gets lumped together with all of your other tax data. Fill out the extra Schedule SE form to determine the amount of self-employment tax owed, and the calculated amount gets carried straight to your 1040.

Just like regular state and federal income tax, self-employment tax is only calculated on your profit (Revenue-Expenses=Profit).

Filing Quarterly Estimated Taxes

Related to self-employment is the need to file Quarterly Estimated tax payments to the IRS.

Most non-business owners file the personal tax return (1040) at the end of the year, and expect to get a little refund or owe a small amount. This was most likely your situation before you started your blogging business.

Owning your own business means that you are earning income throughout the year, and there is no employer sending the IRS your tax withholding with every paycheck. The IRS does not want you to owe them a lot of money at the end of the year, they want their money throughout the year! If you expect to OWE the IRS $1,000 or more when you complete your end of year tax return, you need to start making quarterly estimated tax payments throughout the year.

Form 1040 ES[16] (short for estimated) walks you through calculating how much to pay to the IRS on a quarterly basis, thereby reducing the amount of tax liability you will owe at the end of the year. To reiterate, the 1040 ES is the quarterly form that helps you calculate your estimated taxes to submit to the IRS throughout the year. The 1040 is the tax return you file at the end of every year regardless.

How Much Should I Set Aside for Taxes?

What percentage of your profits should you set aside for taxes each month? The answer is, it varies. One of the hardest concepts to grasp for new business owners is that your business profits and their related tax burdens are combined with your family's overall tax situation. Your family has a unique set of circumstances that determines how much income tax you pay.

For example, let's say your family is in the 25% tax bracket. When you file your 1040 tax return at the end of the year, you will not end up paying 25% of your income in taxes. There are many deductions and calculations that go into each tax return that influence your effective tax rate. Your effective tax rate is the total amount of tax paid, divided by your total income, and is always much lower than your tax bracket. The effective tax rate for each family will be different depending on the various deductions you are able to take.

I have no easy or straightforward answer for you. My recommendation is to perform the estimated tax calculation on form 1040-ES and calculate what percentage of your profits the IRS is asking you to pay that quarter. Use that percentage as a basis for what amount you reserve for future tax payments. At the end of the year you can also adjust your calculated tax reserve based upon the effective tax rate you pay.

Other Self-Employment Concerns

Have you ever heard people comment that starting a business can be a bad financial move because of the self-employment tax? Has your husband or wife voiced concerns that your business will cost the family money in extra taxes? I have certainly heard comments such as these over the years.

It is a big misconception that a small business can negatively impact a family's finances due to the self-employment tax.

If you start a business and make a profit then you will have to pay the self-employment tax (employee and employer portion of the Social Security and Medicare Tax), but the tax is only a percentage of your **business profits.** You have made money from your business, and only on those **profits** is the self-employment tax applied.

If your business loses money - no self-employment tax is owed.

Other income from a regular job - not subject to the self-employment tax.

If your business makes a **profit**, you have more money than you did before, and taxes owed are only a percentage of your profits.

Sometimes new business owners make a little profit, and consequently see their personal income tax refund go down when they file their taxes at the end of the year. A false assumption is then made that their business cost them money.

If your business made a profit, you have more money. If your business is new, or your profits weren't high, you might not have been making quarterly estimated tax payments. You were actually making a profit each month from your small business, but you pocketed all of it without withholding any for taxes.

When the end of the year rolls around and you do your taxes.

You have been enjoying the profits of your business all year without paying taxes on them, and now it's time to pay those taxes.

You complete your Schedule C, the profit is carried over to your 1040, and whoops, the business taxes that haven't been paid all year, now need to be paid to the IRS. Since business and personal taxes get combined, your usual refund amount goes down to pay the business taxes, making it appear that your business cost you money, when in reality it didn't.

Let's look at an example to illustrate. Your new blogging business made a profit of $5,000 during the year, but you didn't know how to handle business profits or taxes, so you didn't pay any taxes throughout the year. For ease of calculation, let's say the taxes attributable to your business amount to $1,000. After taxes, you made an extra $4,000! Yeah!

In past years, before you started your business, your personal tax refund from the IRS was always about $1,500. This year, after you do your taxes, you only get a $500 refund. Yikes! You start to think, "My business cost me money!"

The additional taxes you owed, were on business **profits**. You actually made an extra $4,000 this year which is awesome! It appears as though your business was a big money waster because you waited to pay all your business taxes at the end of the year, thereby reducing your refund.

When other people try to convince you that your hard earned money from your business is costing you and your family money, whip out this handy guide to taxes and give them a little lesson! They are going to be so impressed at your extensive tax knowledge!

11

How to Pay Yourself and Filing Your Tax Return

You have made it this far, reading a book about the most exciting topic around . . . taxes. Don't give up yet, there are just a few more things you may need to know!

How to Pay Yourself from your Business

As a sole-proprietorship or single member LLC you pay yourself from your business by transferring money from your business bank account to your personal bank account. You can do this through an electronic transfer, or by writing a check.

The amount of money you pay yourself is up to you. You can pay yourself as much or as little as you would like. You can also pay yourself at whatever frequency you would like, for example weekly, monthly, or yearly.

The most important thing is to not use your business financial accounts for personal purchases as a means of payment. Don't use your business debit card for your groceries or Starbucks runs, and consider that your form of payment. Transactions like this break down the separation between business and personal finances that we want to maintain.

Does the Amount I Pay Myself Affect My Taxes?

The short answer is no, let me explain. As discussed previously, your business profit or loss is calculated on Schedule C, and that number is carried over to your 1040 to be taxed along with your personal taxes. The business profit or loss is determined by taking your revenue minus your expenses.

Since you are a savvy blogger that reads informative books about your business taxes, I'm guessing you have a business profit for the year (revenues exceeding expenses). The entire business profit is taxed, whether or not you withdrew that money from your business accounts for personal use.

The amount of money that you withdraw from your business for your personal life does not affect the amount of tax you owe at the end of the year. You could withdraw all of your profits at the end of the year, or keep all profits in the business, either way you owe the same amount of taxes.

Shall we look at an example? As a blogger you made $17,000

in revenue and had $5,000 in expenses during the year. Your business profits for the year were $12,000. This is your taxable business income. $12,000 will appear at the bottom of your Schedule C and be carried forward to your 1040.

During the year you transferred $1,000 every month from your business checking account to your personal checking account. You still owe taxes on the $12,000 of business profit.

Or let's say during the year you kept your business profits in your business checking account, but decided to take a family trip in December, and withdrew the $12,000 to pay for your family vacation. You will still owe taxes on the $12,000 of business profit.

OR let's say during the year you kept your business profits in your business checking account and withdrew zero. You will still owe taxes on the $12,000 of business profit.

Withdrawing or not withdrawing your business profits does not affect the amount of taxes you will owe. The tax amount owed remains the same. You are the business, and will be taxed on your business profits, regardless of the way you decide to use those business profits.

Filing Your Tax Return

Throughout this book we have talked about many tax rules and forms! You will probably have nightmares about Schedule C and Form 1040! With all of these rules, forms and schedules, paying someone to do your taxes may seem to be your only option. Not necessarily!

The Blogger's Simple Guide to Taxes has walked you through the important details you need to complete your business taxes with the help of a tax program. There are many great online tax programs such as H&R Block or Turbo Tax, and these programs know what questions to ask, and what forms to fill out. Your job is to know how to answer those questions, and what deductions you can take. Hopefully this book gave you the tools for both.

When you purchase a tax program, make sure you pick one that can do your Schedule C. Many tax programs have various versions. Some versions are only intended for very basic filings, such as just a 1040. Other versions are designed to handle more complicated situations such as the forms required for small business filings. Make sure the tax program version you select will be able to file your Schedule C if you decide to go the tax program route.

If you decide to use a tax accountant or an in person tax service, hopefully this book has educated you on the deductions you can take, and how to properly document your tax deductions. The more informed you are about your small business taxes, the more you can inform your tax accountant of various deductions you qualify for, thereby maximizing your refund.

Conclusion

We are done! Hopefully, it hasn't been too painful learning about the tax and accounting side of your blogging business. For more tax and accounting help, head over to my website, Small Business Sarah(www.SmallBusinessSarah.com). My goal is to take the mystery and misery out of your small business taxes and accounting, and basically be your tour guide through all of this necessary, but not fun, technical information.

You can receive your free Small Business Startup Checklist by signing up for my newsletter[17]. And if you missed your free business mileage tracker in the Blogging Expenses chapter, don't forget to grab it here.

Good luck on your blogging journey!

-Sarah

More From Sarah Korhnak

The Thriving Business Journal: A Guided Journal for reflecting, analyzing, and growing your business

Idea Craft: Discover the Best Small Business Idea for You!

The Etsy Seller's Simple Guide to Taxes: A Time and Money Saving Guide for Makers and Crafters

The VA Tax Guide - A Complete Resource for your Virtual Assistant Business

Notes

INTRODUCTION

1   Find me online at SmallBusinessSarah.com

2   Receive your free Small Business Startup Checklist when you sign-up for my newsletter. https://sbs-media-llc.ck.page/a904f3bb3a

3   Find me on Pinterest at www.Pinterest.com/SmallBizSarah/

SO YOU STARTED A BLOG

4   Nine points to help you determine if you are a hobby or a business. https://www.irs.gov/faqs/small-business-self-employed-other-business/income-expenses/income-expenses

CHOOSING A BUSINESS STRUCTURE

5   Schedule C Profit or Loss From a Business. https://www.irs.gov/pub/irs-pdf/f1040sc.pdf

REGISTERING YOUR BUSINESS

6   Obtaining an EIN. https://sa.www4.irs.gov/modiein/individual/index.jsp

SCHEDULE C

7   Schedule C Profit and Loss from a Business. https://www.irs.gov/pub/irs-pdf/i1040sc.pdf

BLOGGING EXPENSES

8   IRS Publication 535 on Businesses Expenses. https://www.irs.gov/pub/irs-pdf/p535.pdf

TRAVEL EXPENSES

9   IRS guidance on Travel, Entertainment, Gift, and Car Expenses in Publication 463.

https://www.irs.gov/pub/irs-pdf/p463.pdf

10   Publication 463, again!
      https://www.irs.gov/pub/irs-pdf/p463.pdf

11   Current year standard mileage rate.
      https://www.irs.gov/tax-professionals/standard-mileage-rates

12   Free Printable Mileage Tracker. https://sbs-media-llc.ck.page/616d59502f

HOME OFFICE AND QBI TAX DEDUCTIONS

13   Expenses for Business Use of Your Home Form. https://www.irs.gov/pub/irs-pdf/f8829.pdf

14   Business Use of Your Home IRS Guidelines.
      https://www.irs.gov/pub/irs-pdf/p587.pdf

SELF-EMPLOYMENT

15   Self-Employment Tax form Schedule SE.
      https://www.irs.gov/pub/irs-pdf/f1040sse.pdf

16   IRS Form 1040 ES, Estimated Tax for Individuals. https://www.irs.gov/pub/irs-pdf/f1040es.pdf

CONCLUSION

17   Sign up for my newsletter to receive your free Small Business Startup Checklist.
      https://sbs-media-llc.ck.page/a904f3bb3a